HOLIDAYS

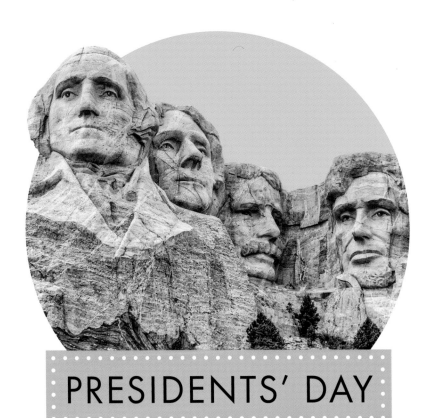

PRESIDENTS' DAY

by Mari Schuh

AMICUS | AMICUS INK

ceremony

parade

Look for these
words and pictures
as you read.

hat

clothes

Many flags fly.
It is Presidents' Day!

Presidents' Day is in February.
It honors U.S. presidents.

ceremony

See the ceremony?

A speech is given.

People listen.

They learn about history.

parade

See the parade?
A band plays.
Colin plays a big drum. Fun!

See the hat?

Leo made it.

It looks like Abraham Lincoln's hat.

hat

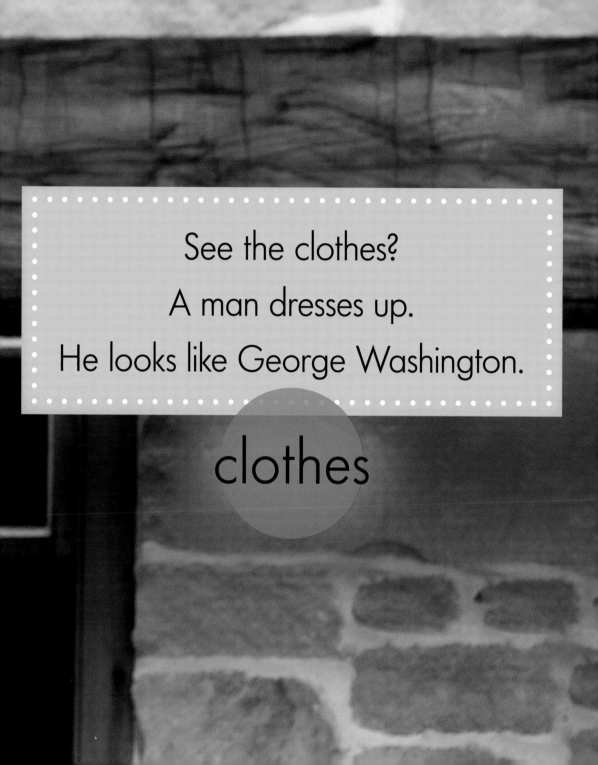

See the clothes?
A man dresses up.
He looks like George Washington.

clothes

Sofia colors a flag.

She learns about the presidents.

ceremony

parade

Did you find?

hat

clothes

Spot is published by Amicus and Amicus Ink
P.O. Box 227, Mankato, MN 56002
www.amicuspublishing.us

Library of Congress Cataloging-in-Publication Data
Names: Schuh, Mari C., 1975- author.
Title: Presidents' Day / by Mari Schuh.
Description: Mankato, MN : Amicus, [2022] | Series:
   Spot holidays | Audience: Ages 4–7 | Audience:
   Grades K–1
Identifiers: LCCN 2019055365 (print) | LCCN 2019055366
   (ebook) | ISBN 9781645491040 (library binding) | ISBN
   9781681526713 (paperback) | ISBN 9781645491460 (pdf)
Subjects: LCSH: Presidents' Day—Juvenile literature. |
   Holidays—Juvenile literature.
Classification: LCC E176.8 .S38 2022 (print) | LCC E176.8
   (ebook) | DDC 394.261—dc23
LC record available at https://lccn.loc.gov/2019055365
LC ebook record available at https://lccn.loc
   gov/2019055366

Alissa Thielges, editor
Deb Miner, series designer
Catherine Berthiaume, book designer
Bridget Prehn, photo researcher

Photos by Shutterstock/Roger Utting
cover, 16, Adventures On Wheels 1,
fstockfoto 3, Sergey-73 4–5, Stuart
Monk 8–9, AlexandraKa 14; Alamy/
Duncan Selby 6–7, B Christopher 12–13;
Getty/Chip Somodevilla 10–11

PRESIDENTS' DAY